If you were an

Exclamation Point

by Shelly Lyons
illustrated by Sara Gray

PICTURE WINDOW BOOKS
Minneapolis, Minnesota

exclamation point (!)

a punctuation mark used to show force or strong feeling

Editors: Christianne Jones and Jill Kalz
Designer: Tracy Davies
Page Production: Melissa Kes
Art Director: Nathan Gassman
Editorial Director: Nick Healy
The illustrations in this book were created with acrylics.

Picture Window Books
151 Good Counsel Drive
P.O. Box 669
Mankato, MN 56002-0669
877-845-8392
www.capstonepub.com

Printed in China.
072010
005830

Library of Congress Cataloging-in-Publication Data
Lyons, Shelly.
If you were an exclamation point / by Shelly Lyons ;
illustrated by Sara Gray.
p. cm. — (Word Fun)
Includes index.
ISBN 978-1-4048-5326-3 (library binding)
ISBN 978-1-4048-5327-0 (paperback)
ISBN 978-1-4048-6707-9 (paperback)
1. English language—Punctuation—Juvenile literature.
2. English language—Exclamations—Juvenile literature.
3. Parades—Juvenile literature. 4. Language arts
(Primary) I. Gray, Sara, ill. II. Title.
PE1450.L94 2009
428.2—dc22   2008039420

Looking for exclamation points? Watch for the **BIG** marks throughout the book.

Special thanks to our advisers for their expertise:

Rosemary G. Palmer, Ph.D., Department of Literacy
College of Education, Boise State University

Terry Flaherty, Ph.D., Professor of English
Minnesota State University, Mankato

If you were an exclamation point ...

3

... you could shout,

"Stand back! Listen! Here comes the marching band!"

5

If you were an exclamation point, you would replace the period at the end of a sentence. An exclamation point shows excitement or emphasis. It shouts, or exclaims.

"The marching band is the best part of the parade!" yells Eliot.

If you were an exclamation point,
you could make a lot of noise.

"Boom!" rumble
the drums.

If you were an exclamation point, you would exclaim something. You could show strong feelings.

123 12

"I love fire trucks!" exclaims Eliot.

"I've always wanted my own hat!" hollers Lou.

If you were an exclamation point, you could make an excited choice.

"Which horse do you like best?" asks Kate.

"That one!" shouts Eliot.

13

If you were an exclamation point, you could help get someone's attention.

"Kate! Over here!"

If you were an exclamation point, you could give a command.

"Go buy some cotton candy! Run!" yells Kate's uncle.

"Don't eat too much!" yells Kate's aunt.

16

If you were an exclamation point, you could show alarm.

"Look out!" yells Eliot.

"Duck!" hollers Kate.

18

Too late!

19

If you were an exclamation point, you could scold. You could also apologize.

"Shame on you!" says Lou.

"Sorry!" says the clown.

21

You would get lots of attention ...

123   123

... if you were an
exclamation point!

22